To God, the greatest painter in the world.
My beautiful family in the present and in the future.

W.F I love you!

Aniceto Pedroso, 2024

THiS BOOK BELONGS TO:

ALL RIGHTS RESERVED 2024

TEST COLOR PAGE

CUCUMBERS

ONION

LETTUCE

EGGPLANT

CABBAGE

SALAD

EGGPLANT

POTATO

TOMATOES

POTATO

ONION